75p

G000294445

POP
BAKERY

POP

Clare O'Connell

BAKERY

25 RECIPES FOR DELICIOUS LITTLE CAKES ON STICKS

CICO BOOKS

LONDON NEW YORK

For Omelie Alice

Published in 2012 by CICO Books
An imprint of Ryland Peters & Small Ltd
519 Broadway, 5th Floor, New York, NY 10012
20-21 Jockey's Fields, London WC1R 4BW
www.cicobooks.com

10 9 8 7 6 5 4 3 2 1

Text © Clare O'Connell 2011, 2012
Design and photography © CICO Books 2011, 2012

The author's moral rights have been asserted.
All rights reserved. No part of this publication
may be reproduced, stored in a retrieval system,
or transmitted in any form or by any means,
electronic, mechanical, photocopying, or otherwise,
without the prior permission of the publisher.

A CIP catalog record for this book is available from
the Library of Congress and the British Library.

The recipes in this book have previously been
published by CICO Books in *POP Bakery*.

ISBN for kit: 978-1-908862-25-9

Printed in China

Editor: Katie Hardwicke
Designer: Paul Tilby
Photographer: Nichole Rees

Cake POP molds

This kit includes two cake POP molds—a bird and
a star. For more information on how to use the
molds, see pages 9 and 11.

Please note that the cake POP molds are not oven
safe or dishwasher safe. Wash the molds before using
them. Not suitable for children.

CONTENTS

introduction

What an honor it is to be doing this book. The past year has been pure madness, full of ridiculously exciting projects. My business, POP Bakery, was born, and still remains, in my childhood home. I was inspired to start POP Bakery because I fell in love with cake POPs, and while babysitting my little friend Sadie one day, I set about creating my own version. People have warmed instantly to these little balls of love. They are impossible not to like, not only aesthetically but more importantly because of their taste—undeniably good!

Having worked in bakeries for the year before founding POP Bakery, and having always had a creative flair when it came to cake decorating, I had finally found the perfect product to utilize both of these loves and talents. Cake POPs have endless scope for creativity. They never get boring—we design new ones practically every week at POP Bakery. They are a dream product to work with as a creative baker, and an even more perfect idea to share in a book! This is POP Bakery's first book, which I hope will inspire the imaginations of lots of aspiring bakers and cake decorators.

The completion of this book confirms all the hopes and dreams I had when starting POP Bakery last year—we can finally say goodbye cupcake and hello POP! A new era has arrived and I hope you enjoy POPping as much as I have over the last year of POP Mania!

Clare O'Connell

POP SHOP

There are a few items that you need to have on hand in order to make your POP-making experience fun and successful. Most are standard pieces of kitchen equipment, but you may need to visit a specialty cake store or search online for some of the more unusual ingredients. Always keep a good supply of lollipop sticks (see Suppliers, page 62).

POP EQUIPMENT

Food processor—for making the cake and the cream cheese frosting, though you can also do both of these by hand.

Microwave—for melting the candy melts.

Accurate measuring scales—to ensure that each POP is the same weight and size.

Lollipop sticks—essential to transform a cake ball into a POP!

Paintbrush—have a selection of sizes, including several with fine tips for delicate details and thicker ones for brushing on dusting powder and glitter.

Edible marker pens—can be used instead of cocoa butter for adding detailing to POPs.

Palette—a plate, porcelain egg cup, or clean paint palette is useful for laying out different colored cocoa butters.

Polystyrene block—this is ideal for standing your POPs in until they set. You can often find polystyrene blocks in protective packaging. Make a few holes in readiness for your dipped POP. A clean tray or colander can also be used.

Cover—lollipop covers (made from cellophane wrap) are available online (see page 62).

Keep your POPs covered if drying and storing in the refrigerator, and cover any pops once they've been dried and removed from the freezer. This will protect your POP and prevent it from sweating. Covered POPs look great gift-wrapped with a twist of ribbon.

Silicon molds—to shape fondant features to attach to your POPs, available in a huge variety of shapes. Insert fondant mixed with gum tragacanth (see below) and let set before applying to your POP.

Cookie cutters—for cutting perfect circles or the fluted

ruff on the clown POPs.

Cake POP molds—these provide an easy way to shape cake balls before dipping them in candy melts. Roll the cake balls as normal, then put them in the refrigerator for about 10 minutes. Press a chilled cake ball into one side of the mold, then close the mold to shape it. Any excess dough can be collected and rolled together to make additional cake balls. Return the molded balls to the refrigerator for a few hours (or the freezer for 10-15 minutes), then follow the normal POPping process (see page 11).

POP INGREDIENTS

Candy melts—are wafers of colored candy that you melt in the microwave to form a liquid paste for dipping. They are available in 14 oz (400 g) packages in a variety of colors. Melt following the package instructions, dip in your POP, and when the coating has set, it makes the perfect base for decoration. Candy melts are available in vanilla or chocolate flavor. Thin with a tablespoon of vegetable oil if the mixture is too thick. These keep well, so if you melt too many, just cover in plastic wrap and keep at

room temperature until your next POPping session.

Cocoa butter—is used by chocolatiers to add detail to intricate confections, and in the POP kitchen for special effects. It can be bought online (see page 62). Before use, melt the cocoa butter by placing the bottle in the microwave for 2-4 minutes, until you can hear the liquid move when you shake the bottle. Pour onto a palette and use as paint.

Dipping solution/rejuvenator spirit—can be mixed with edible dusting powder to paint details on POPs instead of cocoa butter. Clear alcohol or clear

vanilla extract can also be substituted for dipping solution. Use edible glaze spray after painting using dusting powder to prevent smudging.

Sprinkles—there is a huge variety of sprinkles available to transform your POPs!

Food coloring—there are edible pastes, liquids, dusts, glitters, and paints available to suit any project. Edible dusting powders (also known as edible tints) are the most versatile colored powders for decorating your POPs and are best applied with a paintbrush.

Fondant (regal icing)—this thick, ready-made frosting can

be molded into any shape, from little balls for eyes to more detailed shapes using silicon molds. Mix with gum tragacanth (see below) to ensure that your piece hardens and keeps its shape.

Gum tragacanth—is made from natural gum and is mixed with fondant (regal icing) to make a stronger base, ideal for modeling. Add 1-2 teaspoons of the powder to a handful of fondant and mix in with your hands until the fondant feels harder and a little less sticky. You can then mold it into the required shapes, or insert into a silicon mold, and let harden.

BEFORE YOU POP

These are the essential techniques that you must master before you embark on this POPtastic journey. It may take a couple of tries before you get the hang of it, but as we know, practice makes perfect—especially with a wonderful treat like a cake POP.

MAKING THE CAKE

This recipe is for a simple chocolate sponge cake that forms the base for all the POPs.

YOU WILL NEED

1/2 cup (125 g) slightly salted butter, at room temperature

scant 3/4 cup (125 g) superfine (caster) sugar

2 medium eggs

heaped 1 cup (125 g) self-rising flour

2 tablespoons cocoa powder

8 inch (20 cm) cake tin, greased and lined

1 Preheat the oven to 325°F (160°C) Gas Mark 3.

2 Put the butter and sugar in a food processor, and beat on medium speed until white and fluffy.

3 Slowly add the eggs as you continue to beat the mixture. Then sift over the flour and cocoa and continue to mix until everything is well combined.

4 Pour the batter into the prepared cake tin and bake in the preheated oven for 25 minutes, or until risen and cooked through. Test if it's cooked by inserting a skewer; if cooked, the skewer comes out clean.

5 Leave your cake to cool in the tin for 30–40 minutes, then turn out onto a wire cooling rack for a few hours to cool down completely. Even better, make the cake the day before you want to make your POPs.

MAKING
THE CAKE BALLS

Makes 20 POPs
1 cooled cake (see left)
scant ¼ cup (70 g) full-fat cream cheese
1 cup (140 g) confectioner's (icing) sugar, sifted

1 Put the cake in a food processor and process to form a mixture with a crumb-like consistency. Put to one side. Combine the cream cheese and confectioner's (icing) sugar in a food processor until well mixed.

2 Combine the cake crumbs and cream cheese frosting with your hands, until all the frosting is incorporated and you are left with a moist mixture.

3 Measure out 1 oz (30 g) of cake mixture on digital scales. Roll this into a ball and place on a plate. Measure and roll 19 more cake balls.

4 Put the plate of cake balls or molded POP shapes in the refrigerator and let cool for a few hours or, if short on time, in the freezer for 10-15 minutes until hard, but not rock hard or frozen through.

Using cake POP molds
If you are using cake POP molds to shape your cake balls, follow steps 1–3 and then put the cake balls into the refrigerator for 10 minutes to chill before pushing them into the molds (see page 9). Once molded, let them harden in the refrigerator or freezer (see step 4).

CLASSIC POPs

YOU WILL NEED

20 x 1-oz (30-g) cake balls
  (see page 11)
14 oz (400 g) candy melts
1 tablespoon vegetable oil
sprinkles, for decoration

20 lollipop sticks

1 Put the candy melts into a microwavable bowl. Microwave on a medium heat for about 2 minutes, stirring at 30-second intervals to ensure that the candy melts do not burn.

2 Once the candy melts are completely melted, dip ⅓ inch (1 cm) of a lollipop stick into the candy melts, then insert it into the hardened cake ball.

This is how you transform your cake ball into a plain POP—ready for decorating and becoming a thing of wonder!

3 Keep stirring the melts throughout to ensure that they maintain a smooth consistency. If you find they are too thick, thin the mixture with a tablespoon of vegetable oil.

4 Holding the end of the stick, dip the cake POP into the bowl of candy melts, covering the cake POP entirely and using a spoon to help if necessary. Gently shake the cake POP to remove any excess candy melts.

5 If using sprinkles or sugar-based decorations, decorate your POP while the coating is still wet. Insert the end of the stick in a polystyrene block to dry. Cover with cellophane and store in the refrigerator. When dry, add cocoa butter decoration (if using) and let dry in the freezer for 5-10 minutes, before covering and storing in the refrigerator. The POPs will keep for a week in the refrigerator or two days at room temperature.

POP TIP

Don't leave finished POPs in the refrigerator uncovered as they will sweat.

YOU WILL NEED

20 x 1-oz (30-g) cake balls (see page 11)
1 package (14 oz/400 g) each candy melts
  in assorted colors
edible glitter powder
black cocoa butter
vegetable oil

20 lollipop sticks
paintbrush
palette

SKULL
POPs

These were inspired by some amazing neon papier-mâché skulls that I purchased on a trip to Mexico.

1 Shape the cake ball into a skull shape. Try to define the jaw, cheekbones, eye sockets, and forehead.

2 Prepare your first candy melt color (see pages 12–13). Dip ⅓ inch (1 cm) of a lollipop stick into the melt and insert into the base of the skull. Dip the entire skull into the melts until entirely coated. Repeat steps 1–2 with the remaining cake balls, using different colors of melts as preferred. Let set.

3 Dip your finger in the glitter container and press into each eye socket. Melt the black cocoa butter in the microwave on medium heat for 2–4 minutes. Paint on a triangular "nose," "teeth," and a cross, or your chosen design. Let dry in the freezer for 5–10 minutes, then cover and store in the refrigerator.

20 x 1-oz (30-g) cake balls
(see page 11)
1 package (14 oz/400 g)
white candy melts
40 jumbo confetti sprinkles
black cocoa butter

20 lollipop sticks
paintbrush
palette

**These are super cute—the simple features of
a panda's face make them perfect for POPs!**

PANDA
POPs

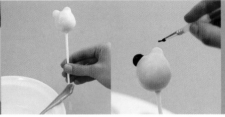

1 Prepare the candy melts (see pages 12-13). While heating the melts, shape each cake ball with your fingers to look like a bear's face by molding a snout. Once the candy melts are ready, take two jumbo confetti sprinkles and dip each one halfway into the melts, then insert them into the top of the head to form the ears.

2 Dip ⅓ inch (1 cm) of a lollipop stick into the candy melts and insert the stick into the bottom of the panda's head. Dip the entire head into the melts until coated entirely with white. Repeat steps 1-2 with the other balls. Leave the panda heads to set in a colander.

3 While they are setting, microwave the black cocoa butter on a medium heat for 2-4 minutes until you can hear the liquid when you shake the bottle. Pour the cocoa butter onto the palette and, using a thin paintbrush, paint the ears.

4 Paint the nose and mouth. Then paint the eyes—paint them as thick black circles, leaving a gap in the middle to dot with a black pupil. Dry the panda POPs in the freezer in a colander or lay on a tray for 5-10 minutes, until no black comes off onto your finger when you touch the paintwork.

One of POP Bakery's most eye-catching POPs
and my personal favorite!

RUSSIAN DOLL
POPs

20 x 1-oz (30-g) cake balls (see page 11)
1 package (14 oz/400 g) white candy melts
colored cocoa butters in black and other colors

20 lollipop sticks
paint palette
thin paintbrush

1 Take your balls from the fridge and split each one into two balls, one bigger than the other for the body. Keep the heads and bodies in the fridge while you prepare the candy melts (see pages 12–13). Once your candy melts are ready, take the heads and bodies from the fridge. Dip the head in the candy melts and attach it securely to the body of the cake POP.

2 Dip ⅓ inch (1 cm) of a lollipop stick into the candy melts and insert it into the bottom of the doll's body. Then dip the entire doll POP into your melts and shake slowly to remove all excess. Leave the doll to set in a colander. Repeat steps 1–2 for the remaining 19 dolls.

3 While they are setting, melt the cocoa butters in the microwave on a medium heat for 2–4 minutes. Then pour them into a palette or the lid of the bottle. Egg cups are also perfect palettes for the paints. Take the paintbrush and first paint on a circle, followed by the hairline, and then the eyes and mouth.

4 Take the other colors and paint the decoration onto your doll. I tend to paint some bodies with flowers and others with hearts. Leave the other side of the dolls unpainted so that you can lay them down on a tray. Place in the freezer to dry for 5–10 minutes.

TOOTH POPs

This cute idea came from a customer who wished to thank a loyal dentist. They make perfect little gifts from the tooth fairy, too!

YOU WILL NEED

20 x 1-oz (30-g) cake balls (see page 11)
1 package (14 oz/400 g) white candy melts
black cocoa butter (optional)

20 lollipop sticks
palette
thin paintbrush or edible marker pen

1 Prepare the candy melts (see pages 12–13). While heating the melts, shape your cake ball into a tooth with roots. This is a simple, squared-off shape with a curved base, creating two "roots" at the outer edges.

2 Dip ⅓ inch (1 cm) of a lollipop stick into the candy melts and insert it into the bottom of the tooth. Dip the entire tooth into the melts until coated with white. Repeat steps 1–2 with the other balls. Leave the teeth POPs to set.

3 Paint a face onto the POPs with an edible marker pen or a paintbrush and black cocoa butter (while they are setting, microwave the cocoa butter on a medium heat for 2–4 minutes, if using). You can give each one its own character—try adding eyelashes for girls! If using cocoa butter, let dry in the freezer for 5–10 minutes; if using a pen, there is no need to leave to dry. Cover and store in the refrigerator.

SNAIL POPs

Snails have such a lovely silhouette, which is number one for a good POP!

YOU WILL NEED

20 x 1-oz (30-g) cake balls (see page 11)
gum tragacanth
white fondant (regal icing)
1 package (14 oz/400 g) each white and
  black candy melts
edible dusting powder in assorted colors
colored cocoa butter

20 lollipop sticks
palette
paintbrush

1 Shape a cake ball into a snail shape, making the body from an elongated oval, resembling an eggplant (aubergine).

2 On the snail's head, shape two antennae by molding and separating the end. Prepare the eyes by mixing a little gum tragacanth with some white fondant, roll pieces into 40 small balls, and let harden.

3 To make a neutral tone, such as gray, for the snail shell, mix white and black candy melts together and prepare as normal (see pages 12–13). Dip ⅓ inch (1 cm) of a lollipop stick into the candy melts and insert it into the bottom of the snail. Dip the entire snail into the melts until well coated. While still wet, place the white balls on the snail's antennae. Repeat steps 1–3 with the other balls. Let set.

4 Decorate the snail shell by brushing it with a mixture of different-colored edible dusting powders. Microwave the cocoa butter on a medium heat for 2–4 minutes and paint the details on the snail, remembering to dot the eyes with black, too. Let dry in the freezer for 5–10 minutes, then cover and store in the refrigerator.

PENGUIN
POPs

Who doesn't love penguins? You could accessorize
a whole family with bow ties for the boys and dainty
eyelashes on the mummy penguin!

YOU WILL NEED

20 x 1-oz (30-g) cake balls
(see page 11)
1 package (14 oz/400 g)
each white and black
candy melts
gum tragacanth
white fondant (regal icing)
edible dusting powder in
red and orange
colored cocoa butter

20 lollipop sticks
palette
paintbrush

1 Prepare the eyes by mixing a little gum tragacanth with some white fondant, roll pieces into 40 small balls, and let harden. Prepare the black candy melts (see pages 12-13). While heating the melts, shape your cake ball into an oval for the body. Dip ⅓ inch (1 cm) of a lollipop stick into the candy melts and insert it into the body. Dip the entire penguin into the black melts until well coated. Attach the white eyes while still wet. Repeat with the other balls. Let set.

2 Prepare the white candy melts (see pages 12-13). When the black melt has set, dip the belly into white candy melts (see Tip below). Let dry.

3 Brush on a red beak and then some orange shading with edible dusting powder. Microwave the cocoa butter on a medium heat for 2-4 minutes and outline the beak and feet, and dot the eyes. Let dry in the freezer for 5-10 minutes, then cover and store in the refrigerator.

POP TIP

To achieve a round white belly, fill a spoon with white candy melts and dip the belly into the spoon rather than the actual bowl. If you go over the desired area, just gently wipe away the excess.

MONSTER POPs

Let your imagination run wild and create a monster collection for Halloween treats that go POP in the night!

YOU WILL NEED

20 x 1-oz (30-g) cake balls (see page 11)
1 package (14 oz / 400 g) candy melts in creepy color of your choice
gum tragacanth
white fondant (regal icing)
colored cocoa butters

20 lollipop sticks
palette
paintbrush
silicon mold for lips (optional)

1 Prepare the candy melts (see pages 12–13). While heating the melts, shape your cake ball into a monsterlike shape. Simple, rounded, or balloonlike shapes work well. Dip ⅓ inch (1 cm) of a lollipop stick into the candy melts and insert it into the body.

2 Mix a little gum tragacanth with some white fondant and prepare the eyes and features for your monster. You can make the lips using a silicon mold. Dip the entire monster into the melts until well coated. Repeat steps 1–2 with the other balls.

3 Attach the features while the coating is still wet. Let set. Microwave the cocoa butter on a medium heat for 2–4 minutes and paint on the pupils of the eyes with black and perhaps some fangs with white cocoa butter. Let dry in the freezer for 5–10 minutes, then cover and store in the refrigerator.

LEOPARD POPs

Inspired by creative nail designers, what could be better than leopard-print cake?

YOU WILL NEED

20 x 1-oz (30-g) cake balls
(see page 11)
1 package (14 oz/400 g)
white candy melts
edible dusting powder in
assorted colors
black cocoa butter

20 lollipop sticks
palette
thin paintbrush

1 Prepare the candy melts (see pages 12-13). Dip ⅓ inch (1 cm) of a lollipop stick into the candy melts and insert it into the cake ball. Dip the entire ball into the white melts until well coated. Repeat with the other balls. Let set.

2 Using the tip of the paintbrush, apply spots of edible dusting powder to the POPs, working your way around the entire cake ball.

3 Microwave the cocoa butter on a medium heat for 2-4 minutes. Paint three dashed lines around each spot to create the leopard print. Keep the marks random to look natural. Let dry in the freezer for 5-10 minutes, then cover and store in the refrigerator.

POP TIP

Painting tiny details requires a steady hand. To help you, try resting your hand on the edge of the table, or supporting your arm on your knee.

TIGER POPs

These were inspired by my favorite childhood book, "The Tiger Who Came to Tea." They're just purrfect for teatime!

YOU WILL NEED

20 x 1-oz (30-g) cake balls (see page 11)
1 package (14 oz/400 g) orange candy melts
jumbo heart sprinkles
white and black cocoa butters

20 lollipop sticks
palette
thin paintbrush

1 Shape the cake balls into a head with a protruding muzzle. Prepare the candy melts (see pages 12-13). Dip a heart sprinkle in the melts and insert into the head so that the point forms an ear. Dip ⅓ inch (1 cm) of a lollipop stick into the candy melts and insert into the head. Repeat for the remaining cake balls.

2 Dip the entire cake POP into the orange candy melts and let set. Microwave the white cocoa butter on a medium heat for 2-4 minutes. Paint on the white markings of the tiger. Let dry.

3 Microwave the black cocoa butter on a medium heat for 2-4 minutes. Paint on the eyes and further markings. Add eyelashes for the girls and a more manly expression on the boys. Let dry in the freezer for 5-10 minutes, then cover and store in the refrigerator.

CACTUS POPs

YOU WILL NEED

20 x 1-oz (30-g) cake balls
  (see page 11)
gum tragacanth
fondant (regal icing) in a
  pretty flower color
1 package (14 oz/400 g)
  green candy melts
black cocoa butter

*silicon mold for flowers
  (optional)*
20 lollipop sticks
palette
paintbrush

1 Mix a little gum tragacanth with some white fondant and make some flowers, either molding the shapes by hand or using a silicon mold. Separate the cake ball into three pieces. Shape all three into sausage shapes for the main body and arms of the cactus. Keep the pieces in the refrigerator while you prepare the candy melts (see pages 12–13).

2 Dip the arms into the green candy melts and stick on the sides of the cactus body. Dip ⅓ inch (1 cm) of a lollipop stick into the candy melts and insert it into the cake ball.

3 Dip the whole cactus into the candy melts. Whilst still wet, attach some fondant flowers and let set. Repeat steps 1–3 with the other balls. Microwave the cocoa butter on a medium heat for 2–4 minutes. Paint on the spikes of the cactus with random dashes. Let dry in the freezer for 5–10 minutes, then cover and store in the refrigerator.

POP TIP

To make the fondant flowers even prettier and give them a little more depth, try brushing on some edible dusting powder.

CLOWN POPs

YOU WILL NEED

20 x 1-oz (30-g) cake balls
  (see page 11)
fondant (regal icing) in
  white and red
gum tragacanth
1 package (14 oz/400 g)
  white candy melts
7 oz (200 g) candy melts in
  assorted colors
colored cocoa butter in red,
  white, and black
edible dusting powder

20 lollipop sticks
1 1/4 inch (3 cm) diameter
  fluted cookie cutter
palette
paintbrush or edible
  marker pen

Super fun for any circus-themed party. Go OTT with accessories, expressions, and personalities to vary each character as much as possible.

1 Start by making the POP accessories. Harden your fondant with gum tragacanth (see page 9) and shape a few pieces into cone hats for the clowns. Add contrasting colored fondant balls for the pompoms on the hat. You could also leave them white and paint on patterns with edible dusting powder and cocoa butter. Prepare 20 red noses for the clowns from the hardened fondant.

2 Prepare the candy melts (see pages 12-13). Break a piece off a cake ball and roll it into two small pieces to form the fluff of hair on either side of the clown's head. Dip in some melts and attach to the top of the cake ball. To add a ruffle collar, use a fluted cookie cutter to cut out a piece of flattened cake ball to the same diameter as the head. Attach with candy melts. Dip ⅓ inch (1 cm) of a lollipop stick into the candy melts and insert it into the cake ball, through both the ruff and halfway through the head.

3 Dip the whole clown into the white melts, then attach a red nose and hat, if using, while still wet. Let set. Repeat steps 2-3 for the other cake balls.

4 Using a brush, paint colored candy melt over the hair. Let dry, then repeat to create a thick, hairlike texture. Use edible dusting powder for cheeks and eyes. Microwave the cocoa butter on a medium heat for 2-4 minutes. Mix red and white cocoa butter to make pink for the mouth and paint on a sausage-shaped smile. Using an edible marker pen or black cocoa butter, paint on a cross for eyes, and once the sausage smile is dry, paint a thin black line in the middle to define the lips. Let dry in the freezer for 5-10 minutes, then cover and store in the refrigerator.

FROG POPs

This POP is dedicated to my mum who has a bit of a frog fetish! Simple to make, this little frog chorus will bring a smile to your face.

YOU WILL NEED

20 x 1-oz (30-g) cake balls (see page 11)
white fondant (regal icing)
gum tragacanth
1 package (14 oz/400 g) green candy melts
black cocoa butter (optional)

20 lollipop sticks
palette
paintbrush or edible marker pen

1 First, make the white bulbous eyes using pieces of fondant. Mix some gum tragacanth into the fondant (see page 9) before you start, so that the eyes harden and stay in shape. Roll out 40 eyes and put to one side. Prepare the candy melts (see pages 12–13). Dip ⅓ inch (1 cm) of a lollipop stick into the candy melts and insert it into the cake ball.

2 Dip the whole POP into the green melts, then attach the eyes on the top while still wet. Repeat steps 1–2 for the other cake balls. Let set.

3 Using an edible marker pen or a thin paintbrush and cocoa butter (microwave the cocoa butter on a medium heat for 2–4 minutes, if using), carefully paint dots on the fronts of the eyes and add a cute smile and two nostrils to the face. If using cocoa butter, let dry in the freezer for 5–10 minutes; if using a pen, there is no need to leave to dry. Once dry, cover and store in the refrigerator.

CUPCAKE POPs

Cupcakes are always POPular! These pretty POPs are perfect for girly girls—candy colors and delicate sprinkles are a must!

YOU WILL NEED

20 x 1-oz (30-g) cake balls (see page 11)
1 package (14 oz / 400 g) white candy melts for base
7 oz (200 g) candy melts in assorted colors for the tops
sugar decorations, such as sprinkles, flowers, glitter

20 lollipop sticks
1 1/4 inch (3 cm) diameter fluted cookie cutter
palette
paintbrush

1 Squash your cake ball until it is the same height as your cookie cutter. Cut out a fluted shape. Re-roll the leftover cake ball pieces to make a pattie shape.

2 Prepare the candy melts (see pages 12–13). Dip the base of the pattie into the white candy melts and attach to the base of the cupcake. Dip 3/4 inch (2 cm) of a lollipop stick into the candy melts and insert it all the way through the base and halfway into the top of the cupcake.

3 Dip the whole POP into the white candy melts. Repeat steps 1–3 for the remaining cake balls. Let set. When dry, dip the top of the cupcake POP into a colored melt and attach a sugar flower or sprinkles while wet. Add glitter, if you wish. Cover and store in the refrigerator.

WEDDING CAKE POPs

These delightful POPs are a perfect alternative to a tiered wedding cake. Rather than cutting the cake, why not pose for a POP photo with arms entwined as you would with glasses of champagne?

YOU WILL NEED

20 x 1-oz (30-g) cake balls (see page 11)
1 package (14 oz/400 g) white candy melts
white nonpareils or hundreds and thousands
jumbo sprinkles, hearts, and doves

1 1/4 inch (3 cm) diameter fluted cookie cutter
1 inch (2.5 cm) diameter plain cookie cutter
5/8 inch (1.5 cm) diameter plain cookie cutter
20 lollipop sticks

1 Make the tiers for the cake by flattening your cake ball, then cut the largest, fluted shape first. Re-roll the ball, flatten, and cut out the middle tier. Re-roll the leftovers, flatten, and cut out the smallest tier. Repeat for the remaining cake balls.

2 Prepare the candy melts (see pages 12–13). Dip the bases of the top and middle section in the melted candy melt and stack the three sections on top of each other to create a tiered effect.

3 Dip 3/4 inch (2 cm) of a lollipop stick into the candy melts and insert it three-quarters of the way through the cake, so that all three tiers are attached. Dip the entire POP into the candy melts, sprinkle on nonpareils and insert a jumbo heart or dove on the top. Cover and store in the refrigerator.

POP TIP

You can customize your wedding cake POPs in so many ways with the huge variety of decorations that are available: a pretty sugar rose on the top or mini heart sprinkles would look lovely, and, of course, you can choose different colored melts for the tiers for a less traditional version.

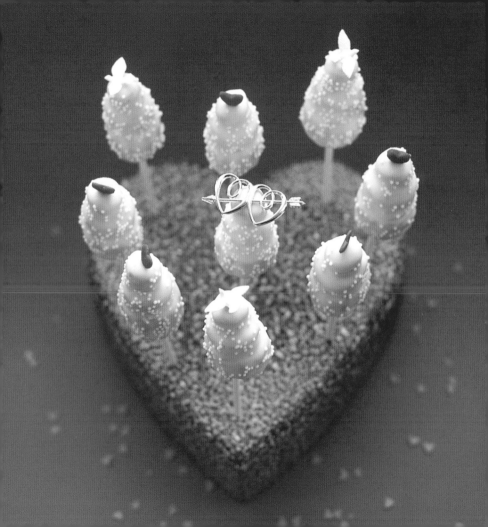

GEISHA POPs

These beautiful POPs were created for a Japanese friend. You could make a lovely Far Eastern display with geishas and origami shapes.

1 Split each cake ball into three balls: one large for the body; one medium for the head; and one small for the hair. Keep the balls in the refrigerator while you prepare the candy melts (see pages 12–13).

2 Dip the base of the head in the candy melts and attach it securely to the body. Dip the hair in the melt and attach it to the head, positioned at the top but angled toward the back. Dip ⅓ inch (1 cm) of a lollipop stick into the candy melts and insert it into the cake ball, through the body and halfway through the head. Dip the entire POP into the white candy melts. Repeat steps 1–2 for the remaining cake balls. Let set.

3 Prepare some black candy melts and dip the hair and top of the head so that the hair appears longer at the sides, suggesting a center parting. Insert two sugar strands for the chopsticks in the hair, while still wet. Let dry.

4 Once dry, brush edible dusting powder onto the cheeks and add pretty colors on the kimono. Microwave the cocoa butter on a medium heat for 2–4 minutes. Using a thin paintbrush, carefully fill in the detail on the face and kimono with black, adding red geisha-like lips—an inverted triangle of three dots gives a good shape. Let dry in the freezer for 5–10 minutes, then cover and store in the refrigerator.

YOU WILL NEED

20 x 1-oz (30-g) cake balls
  (see page 11)
1 package (14 oz/400 g)
  each white and black
  candy melts
white sugar strands
edible dusting powder
black and red cocoa butter

20 lollipop sticks
palette
thin paintbrush

MAYA DOLL POPs

This is a very special POP for my very dear friend Maya, who is an integral part of POP Bakery and a true POPstar!

YOU WILL NEED

20 x 1-oz (30-g) cake balls (see page 11)
1 package (14 oz/400 g) each colored candy melts in exotic colors, such as orange and lime green, plus camel color for skin tones
black and red cocoa butter

20 lollipop sticks
palette
thin paintbrush

1 Split each cake ball into two balls, one bigger than the other for the body. Keep the heads and bodies in the refrigerator while you prepare the candy melts (see pages 12–13). Dip the base of the head in the candy melts and attach it securely to the body of the cake POP.

2 Dip ⅓ inch (1 cm) of a lollipop stick into the candy melts and insert it into the cake ball, through the body and halfway through the head. Dip the entire POP into the colored candy melts. Repeat steps 1–2 for the remaining cake balls. Let set.

3 Prepare the camel-colored melts and dip the side of the head into the melts for the faces (see Tip on page 25). Let set. Microwave the cocoa butter on a medium heat for 2–4 minutes. Using a thin paintbrush, carefully paint details on the saris, closed eyes, and a tiny red bindi on the forehead. A nose chain looks super cute, too! Let dry in the freezer for 5–10 minutes, then cover and store in the refrigerator.

POP TIP

For the sari, outline the face in black and continue the line across the top of the body to suggest the fold in the fabric. Paisley patterns and other Indian designs will bring your lovely Indian dolls to life!

OWL POPS

You can have great fun creating the vibrant plumage on these owls with exotic combinations of edible dusting powder.

20 x 1-oz (30-g) cake balls (see page 11)
1 package (14 oz/400 g) each colored candy melts, such as pale blue or orange
edible dusting powder
white and black cocoa butter

20 lollipop sticks
palette
thin paintbrush

1 Prepare the candy melts (see pages 12-13). While heating the melts, shape your cake ball into an owl shape—start with a fat rectangle and gently flatten the top in the center so that the sides are raised to resemble the peaks of the ears. Dip ⅓ inch (1 cm) of a lollipop stick into the candy melts and insert it into the body.

2 Dip the entire owl POP into the melts and let set. Repeat steps 1-2 for the remaining cake balls. Microwave the white cocoa butter on a medium heat for 2-4 minutes. Paint on the white eyes and let dry before adding the decoration.

3 Coat the body of the owl with edible dusting powder—no strict rules here, just think up interesting color combos and have fun with some shading! Microwave the black cocoa butter on a medium heat for 2-4 minutes. Paint on the final details of the eyes and beak. Let dry in the freezer for 5-10 minutes, then cover and store in the refrigerator.

TOADSTOOL POPs

These are lovely for fairy fans—you can perch little toy fairies on top, or serve them at an Alice in Wonderland-themed tea party.

YOU WILL NEED

20 x 1-oz (30-g) cake balls (see page 11)
1 package (14 oz/400 g) each white and red candy melts
white cocoa butter

20 lollipop sticks
palette
thin paintbrush

1 Shape a toadstool stalk from your cake ball. Next, shape the cap, ensuring it has a flat base and rounded top. Prepare the white candy melts (see pages 12-13) and stick the stalk to the cap. Dip ⅓ inch (1 cm) of a lollipop stick into the candy melts and then insert it into the stalk and halfway into the cap.

2 Dip the entire toadstool POP into the white candy melts and let set. Repeat steps 1-2 for the remaining cake balls.

3 When the white coating has set, prepare the red candy melts. Dip the top part—the cap—into the red melts. Let set. Microwave the white cocoa butter on a medium heat for 2-4 minutes. Paint on white spots. Let dry in the freezer for 5-10 minutes, then cover and store in the refrigerator.

POSH PIG POPs

What a delightful posh pig family, posing for a family photo. Little do they know they are being sold in a butcher's store!

YOU WILL NEED

20 x 1-oz (30-g) cake balls
   (see page 11)
1 package (14 oz/400 g)
   pink candy melts
red jumbo heart sprinkles
white, red, and black cocoa
   butter

20 lollipop sticks
palette
thin paintbrush

1 Shape a snout on your cake ball by molding a rounded point at the front. Prepare the pink candy melts (see pages 12–13). For the ears, dip a jumbo heart into the melts and then insert into the head so that the point protrudes. Dip ⅓ inch (1 cm) of a lollipop stick into the candy melts and insert it into the head.

2 Dip the entire POP pig in the pink candy melts and let set. Repeat steps 1–2 for the remaining cake balls.

3 Microwave the white and red cocoa butter on a medium heat for 2–4 minutes. Mix white and red together in your palette and paint on some pink cheeks and the tip of the snout. Using white, add the eyes and use red for a cheeky smile. Let dry.

4 Prepare the black cocoa butter and paint on the eyes, moustaches, and spectacles—these are not primitive pigs, but posh ones! Let dry in the freezer for 5–10 minutes, then cover and store in the refrigerator.

YOU WILL NEED

20 x 1-oz (30-g) cake balls
(see page 11)
1 package (14 oz/400 g)
each assorted colored
candy melts
red jumbo heart sprinkles
(optional)
black and white cocoa
butter
edible dusting powder
edible glitter powder

bird cake POP mold
20 lollipop sticks
palette
thin paintbrush

1 Shape your cake ball into a bird figure. You can use the bird cake POP mold (see page 9) or mold it with your hands—start with a sausage shape with one fat end, bend upward to create the head, rounding the top, and flatten the opposite end to shape the tail. Prepare the candy melts (see pages 12-13)—you can mix white and black together to make a neutral gray. For a more pronounced beak, dip a jumbo heart sprinkle into the melts and insert it into the head. Dip ⅓ inch (1 cm) of a lollipop stick into the candy melts and insert it into the body of the bird.

2 Dip the entire bird POP into the melts and let set. Repeat steps 1-2 for the remaining cake balls.

3 Microwave the white and black cocoa butters on a medium heat for 2-4 minutes. Paint on white dots for the eyes first, let dry, then add black dots for the pupils. Brush the bird with lovely shades of edible dusting powder and some glitter. Finally, paint on the details of the eyes, beak, and wings. Let dry in the freezer for 5-10 minutes, then cover and store in the refrigerator.

For the peacock, use a basic bird shape but flatten and fan the tail. Have fun with painting the tail pattern!

BIRDIE
POPs

What a lovely menagerie—and great fun to decorate with edible dusting powder! I particularly enjoyed making the peacock POP.

STARFISH
POPs

A POP for all beach-lovers and ideal for beach-themed parties.

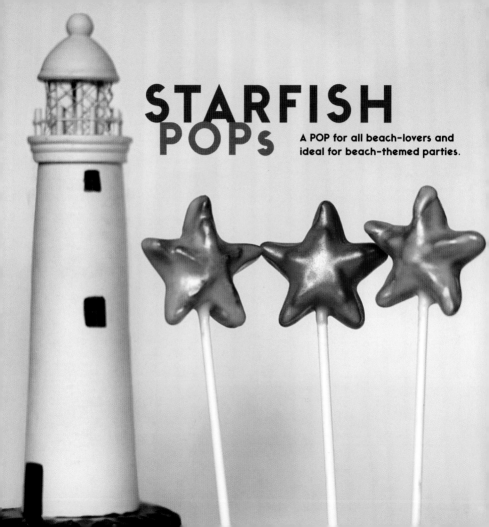

YOU WILL NEED

1 recipe cake ball mixture (if using a star-shaped cookie cutter) or 20 x 1-oz (30-g) cake balls (see page 11)
1 package (14 oz/400 g) each candy melts in assorted colors, such as peach and lemon
edible dusting powder

rolling pin and star-shaped cookie cutter, or star cake POP mold
20 lollipop sticks
palette
thin paintbrush

1 If you have a star-shaped cookie cutter, roll out your cake ball mixture and cut out 20 star shapes (or as many as required). Prepare the candy melts (see pages 12-13) and add little flattened balls of the mixture to the star, to build up the detail, and attach with candy melts. Alternatively, make 20 cake balls and use the star cake POP mold to shape them (see page 9). Dip ⅓ inch (1 cm) of a lollipop stick into the candy melts and insert it between two points of the star. Repeat with the remaining starfish and sticks.

2 Let dry in the freezer for about 10 minutes to make sure the starfish POPs all harden up well and keep their shape when they are dipped. Dip the entire starfish POPs in the candy melts and let set.

3 Use edible dusting powder to shade and decorate the starfish, defining the details of the raised ridges. Cover and store in the refrigerator.

POP TIP

If you notice the shape has heated up while being in your hands, simply pop it in the freezer to harden up for 10-15 minutes before dipping in the candy melts. This is especially useful for POPs with a tricky shape, like the Starfish or Elephants (see page 60).

MARBLE POPs

These marvellous marbles are perfect for fans of the traditional child's game.

YOU WILL NEED

20 x 1-oz (30-g) cake balls (see page 11)
1 package (14 oz/400 g) each candy melts in three contrasting colors

20 lollipop sticks

1 Prepare the candy melts (see pages 12–13) in separate bowls. Dip ⅓ inch (1 cm) of a lollipop stick into a candy melt and insert it into the bottom of a cake ball. Dip your POP into the first color and shake gently to remove any excess melts.

2 Use a spoon to drizzle over the next color, turning the POP so that the pattern blends well into the base color.

3 Use a different spoon to drizzle over the third color, turning as in step 2.

4 Hold the POP upside down over a plate and shake it so that the colors combine to create a marbled effect. Repeat steps 1–4 for the remaining cake balls. Let set. Cover and store in the refrigerator.

POP TIP

The more contrasting the colors, the more effective the marble POP—black and white are particularly dramatic!

FRUIT
POPS

Here, I show you how to make the watermelon, but you could make a whole fruit salad from kiwis, bananas, pineapples, strawberries—just use your imagination!

YOU WILL NEED

20 x 1-oz (30-g) cake balls (see page 11)
1 package (14 oz/400 g) each red, white, and green candy melts
black cocoa butter

20 lollipop sticks
palette
paintbrush

1 Shape a cake ball into a triangle with a rounded base, while you prepare the red candy melts (see pages 12–13). Dip ⅓ inch (1 cm) of a lollipop stick into the candy melts and insert into the POP. Dip the entire POP into the red candy melts. Repeat for the remaining cake balls. Let set.

2 Prepare the white candy melts. Dip the side of the POP into the candy melt. Let set.

3 Prepare the green candy melts. Dip the white edge into the green candy melts for the outer skin, almost covering the white but leaving a rim of white (see Tip on page 25). Let set. Microwave the black cocoa butter on a medium heat for 2–4 minutes and paint little dots for the seeds. Let dry in the freezer for 5–10 minutes, then cover and store in the refrigerator.

ELEPHANT
POPs

POP Circus comes to town!
These are the most
adventurous POPs yet and will
challenge your sculpting skills,
but the results are fantastic!

YOU WILL NEED

20 x 1-oz (30-g) cake balls
  (see page 11)
1 package (14 oz/400 g)
  each elephant-colored
  candy melts, such as gray-
  lilac or pale blue
white, red, and black cocoa
  butter
edible dusting powder,
  including gold

20 lollipop sticks
palette
paintbrush

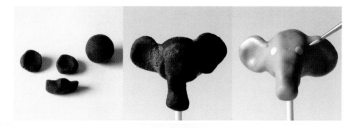

1 Make up the parts of
your elephant from one
cake ball: two ears from
flattened disks, a cylinder
shaped trunk, and
rounded head.

2 Prepare the candy
melts (see pages 12-13).
Attach the features
together using candy
melts. Leave the complete
head in the freezer for at
least 5 minutes to harden
before dipping. Dip ⅓ inch
(1 cm) of a lollipop stick
into the candy melts and
insert into the head.
Repeat steps 1-2 for the
remaining cake balls.

3 Dip the entire POP in the candy melts and let set.
Microwave the white cocoa butter on a medium heat
for 2-4 minutes and paint the eyes white. When dry,
add shading with edible dusting powder to the ears
and end of the trunk. Powder the headdress and
outline it with a little gold edible dusting powder and
water mixed together—this creates a sharp detail of
gold that looks lovely. Microwave the red and black
cocoa butters on a medium heat for 2-4 minutes. Dot
the eyes, and add eyelashes and nostrils, along with a
little red mouth. Let dry in the freezer for 5-10 minutes,
then cover and store in the refrigerator.

SUPPLIERS

All of the equipment and ingredients used to make cake POPs can be bought from cake decorating suppliers. Be aware that new ingredients appear all the time, so if you spend time browsing in cake supply stores, you'll pick up new ideas and inspiration.

Pop Bakery
www.popbakery.co.uk
The home of POP Bakery and a great place for inspiration!

Cake Art (US)
www.cakeart.com
For lollipop sticks, covers, candy melts, brushes, edible dusting powder, cutters, and sprinkles.

Make a Wish Cake Shop (UK)
www.makeawishcakeshop.co.uk
For twist ties, wrappings, lollipop sticks, covers, and sprinkles.

Sugarshack (UK)
www.sugarshack.co.uk
For lollipop sticks, covers, candy melts, brushes, edible dusting powder, cutters, and sprinkles.

Hobbycraft (UK)
www.hobbycraft.co.uk
For candy melts and lollipop sticks.

Wilton (US)
www.wilton.com
For candy melts, lollipop sticks and covers, and sprinkles.

Cake, Cookies, & Crafts (UK)
www.cakescookiesandcraftsshop.co.uk
For jumbo sprinkles and gum tragacanth.

Jesters Cake Supply (US)
www.fondantsource.com
For cocoa butter.

Home Chocolate Factory (UK)
www.homechocolatefactory.com
For cocoa butter.

Chef Rubber (US)
www.chefrubber.com
For cocoa butter.

Sugarcraft (US)
www.sugarcraft.com
For cocoa butter.

Squires Kitchen (UK)
www.squires-shop.com
For gum tragacanth.

Knightsbridge PME (UK)
www.cakedecoration.co.uk
For candy melts and lollipop sticks and covers.

The Party Party Shop (UK)
www.ppshop.co.uk
For dipping solution/rejuvenator spirit, lollipop sticks, and candy melts.

INDEX

ACKNOWLEDGMENTS

With many thanks to Jason, for your help and guidance
in the early days of POP Bakery; Michael and my family,
for being the most supportive and encouraging family
a girl could wish for; Nichole and Marcus, for your lovely
photos and expertise; and Maya, a true POP artist.